PIGEON KEEPING

A GUIDE ON HOW TO REAR HEALTHY PIGEONS

By Lucky James

Table of Contents

Chapter one: Introduction to Pigeon farming

Starting a pigeon farm is one of the most interesting and profitable livestock business. One of the birds that are really considered as a symbol of peace is pigeon. Today a lot of people that has facilities in their homes like to raise pigeons. One good thing about starting a pigeon farm is that it does not require so much labor and investment. You can even raise pigeons at your own leisure time. The baby pigeon meat is called squab. This baby pigeon meat (squab) is very tasty, nutritious and restorative. In fact the meat really has a high demand and price in the market. Another good thing about starting a pigeon farm is that it can really be a great source of some extra income and entertainment.

One thing about pigeon is that if you raise them in a modern way is more profitable than when you raise them in a traditional way. In that case if you actually want to achieve a successful pigeon farm you need to raise your pigeons using modern rearing techniques and also take good care of them very well. Raising pigeons has a lot of advantage. The following are some of the benefits of pigeon farming.

1. Without been told pigeons are known to be a domestic birds that are very easy to handle.

2. One good benefit of pigeon farming is that pigeons lay their eggs as from six months of age and they produce two baby pigeon per month on an average.
3. Another benefit of pigeon raising is that pigeons can be raised in the home yard and also on the roof of the house.
4. In pigeon farming, hatching their eggs take just about 18 days.
5. Another benefit of starting a pigeon farm is that the baby pigeon which is called squab can become suitable for consumption within 3 to 4 weeks of their age.
6. The pigeon house can be built in a small place with little money.
7. The cost of feeding pigeon is very low. Pigeons can collect food by themselves.
8. Another benefits of pigeon farming is that there meat is very tasty and nutritious. The meat also has a great value and demand in the market.
9. Like I said earlier pigeon farming is very entertaining, you can even catch your fun by watching there activities.

10.   Pigeon farming is a business you can make a lot of profit by investing little capital.

11.   Compare to other birds, disease are comparatively less in pigeons.

12.   The droppings from pigeons are really a good source of manure for plants.

13.   The feathers of pigeons can be use to make different types of toys.

14.   One thing about pigeons is that they help to keep the environment clean by eating different types of insects.

15.   Another good benefit of pigeon farming is that pigeons can start laying their eggs when there are about 5 to 6 months of age.

Chapter two: Different types of Pigeon breeds

On this chapter we are going to look at the different types of pigeon breeds. The following are some of the different types of pigeon breeds.

1. The Frillback pigeon breed: This particular breed descended from rock pigeons. Below are the images of this particular breed.

2. **The Barb pigeon breed:** This particular breed has actually been around for a long period in England for about 16th. One notable thing about this breed is the wattling around the eyes. Below is the image of the breed.

3. **The Ice pigeon breed:** This particular breed got some of its unique look due to the powder down that covers the feathers in a whitish dust. Below are the images of the breed.

4. The Brunner pouter pigeon breed: This particular breed actually looks as if they want to walk with their chest because there chest is very high. Below is the image of the breed.

5. The English pouter pigeon breed: This particular breed is a big larger than the Brunner. This breed has a nice long leg and a

long slender body. Below is the image of the breed.

6. The Pigmy pouter pigeon breed: This particular breed is not so popular like the other breeds. This breed is about 12 inches tall. Below is the image of the breed.

7. The English short-faced tumbler pigeon breed: This particular breed head is large, broad, lofty and round. The breed is also short. The shortness of this breed makes it look like a cartoon. Below are the images of this breed.

8. The English carrier pigeon breed: This particular breed is known for is huge eye ceres and wattling around the beak. Below is the image of the breed.

9. The Oriental frill pigeon breed: In the area
   of appearance the Oriental frill pigeon
   breed looks like parrot. This particular breed

was develop in turkey. Below is the image of this breed.

10.   The English trumpeter pigeon breed: This particular breed is the most popular breed in United States. This breed has a fancy feather around is head and it also has a multiple long feathers on its feet. Below is the image of the breed.

11.   The German Modena pigeon breed: The German Modena pigeon breed looks like a chicken. This particular breed originated from Italy and was later imported to Germany in the 18th century. Below is the image of The German Modena pigeon breed.

12. The Capuchin red pigeon breed: This particular breed is similar to the Jacobin pigeon. This breed color is very interesting. Below is the image of the breed.

13.   The Saxon fairy swallow pigeon breed: The Saxon fairy swallow pigeon breed sports extraordinary feathers on its feet. This breed has the same coloring which includes the little splash of color on top of its head. Below is the image of this breed.

14.   The African owl pigeon breed: This particular breed was named after the raptors that have round heads and short beaks. This breed has a ball shape head. Below is the image of this breed.

15.   The Nun pigeon breed: The Nun pigeon breed got its name from its coloring. This particular breed body are all white except for a colored head and bib. The Nun pigeon breed has a distinctive "shell crest" of upturned feathers along the back of the neck. Below is the image of the Nun pigeon breed.

Chapter three: Pigeon housing

One thing about pigeons is that they need a living space that is even more than a cage. If you are actually rearing pigeons either for hobby or for commercial purpose you really need to give them a substantial shelter. If you are building a simple pigeon house you must construct it in a solid way and also the house must be off the ground. A pigeon house can be built with building materials that can be found in your local hardware store. The following are step by step guide on how to build a pigeon house.

First step: You can start by using your protractor to measure an 18.2-degree bevel right along an 8-inch edge of your roof piece. Make sure you mark it with a pencil and use your handsaw to cut the bevel. Then make sure you sand the edge with fine-grit sandpaper.

Second step: The next thing to do is to measure another 18.2-degree angle along the top side piece using a protractor. Make sure that it is 6-inch side opposite your 4.5-inch side. The next thing to do again is to use a handsaw to cut through the angle and sand it with your sandpaper. Make sure you do the same for the bottom piece.

Third step: The next thing to do is to use a hot glue to attach the 4.5-inch edge of the side piece to the 7-inch edge of your floor piece. Make sure you see to it that the 90-degree angle of your side piece is at the floor's corner. The next thing is to use a hammer and a few nails to nail the side in place. Make sure you do the same with your remaining side piece for the other 7-inch edge of your floor.

Fourth step: The next thing to do is to use a hot glue to attach the roof to the sides' top edges. Make sure you see to it that the 18.2-degree beveled edge of your roof is in line with the sides' back edges and also make sure that it has created a flat surface for you to attach the back piece in your next step. Ensure that the roof is slope down over the platform's front.

Fifth step: The next thing to do is to nail the roof in its place with nails and a hammer.
Sixth step: The next thing is to lay your platform on its front, with its face down. Then you have to apply a hot glue around the roof's back edges, floor and sides. Make sure that the house's back piece is extended 2 inches above your roof and below your platform's floor.

Seventh stage: The next thing is to nail the platform to your back piece. Then you need to set it upright with its open front facing forward with your platform's floor standing parallel to the ground.
The following mentioned above are the 7 steps on how to build a pigeon house.

Chapter four: Feeding the pigeon

Pigeon is like any other poultry birds that need a complete balance diet of carbohydrates, proteins, fat, vitamins, minerals and water. The following are some of the varieties of what pigeon eat; greens, berries, fruits, grains and also they occasionally eat things like snail, insects and earthworms.

Try and feed the pigeons with a well balance diet all the time. If by paraventure you are encountering any problem with your pigeon diet or health try as much as possible to consult a veterinarian.

Below is a chart of balance feed for pigeons

Pigeon feed ingredients	Amount of feed in Kg
1. Mustard	1.0 kg
2. Salt	0.4 kg
3. Broken wheat	2.8 kg
4. Broken gram	1.0 kg
5. Broken maize	2.2 kg
6. Soya bean cake	0.8 kg
7. Rice bran	1.8 kg

The total is 10 kg

The following are the major points you need to remember when feeding your pigeons.

1. Try as much as possible to always monitor the amount of food eaten by each pigeon every day.
2. Make sure you always offer fresh water to the pigeon every day.
3. Try as much as possible to always offer a variety of fresh food every day.
4. Make sure that you offer the pigeon's fresh fruit and vegetables every day.
5. Make sure that you clean all food and water dishes daily.

Chapter five: Egg incubation in pigeon

One thing about pigeons is that they lay there first egg after ten days of mating. The pigeon will not sit on the egg all the time unless the outside is very cold. Pigeons normally lay there second egg after skipping a day. After laying the second egg she will now be very ready to incubate both eggs.

During the period of mating you will observe that there are some leftover foods on the trough. The reason is because the pigeon will sit tight on their eggs or squeakers. Make sure you leave the feed on trough, because they will later go back and eat the food.

Chapter six: pigeon disease and treatment

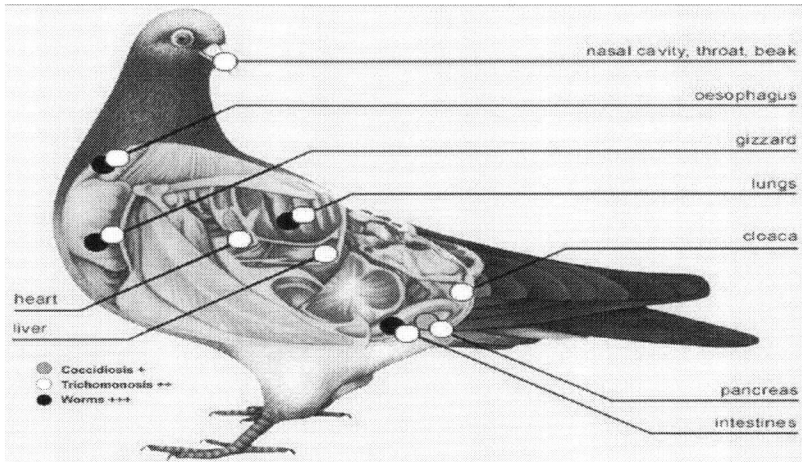

nasal cavity, throat, beak

oesophagus

gizzard

lungs

cloaca

heart

liver

Coccidiosis +
Trichomonosis ++
Worms +++

pancreas

intestines

On this chapter we are going to look at some of the disease that affects pigeons and how to tackle them. The following are some of the diseases that affect pigeons and how to tackle them:

1. The paratyphoid Salmonella bacteria:

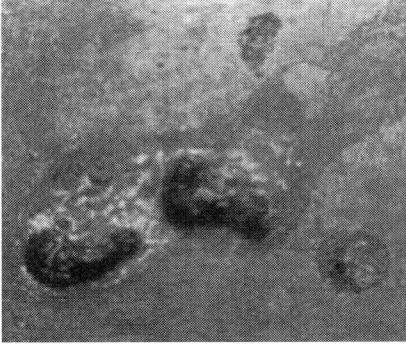

This particular infection is caused by un-sanitary conditions of pigeons and the contamination of the pigeon feed by rodents. This particular infection normally occurs when you are introducing a new pigeons into the loft, without checking first if they are really healthy. Some of the symptoms of Paratyphoid include loss of weight, swelling of the leg and wing, green slimy droppings, etc. The symptoms also include infertile eggs, and one eye blindness. The following are products for prevention and cure.

- You can use furaltadone & Colistine 5% (DAC)
- You can also use trimethoprim ? Sulfa (DAC)
- You can use parastop (Belgica-DeWeerd)
- You can use Parastop (Pantex)
- You can use Sal-Bac Vaccine (Bio-Mune)

2. The Paramyxovirus infection:

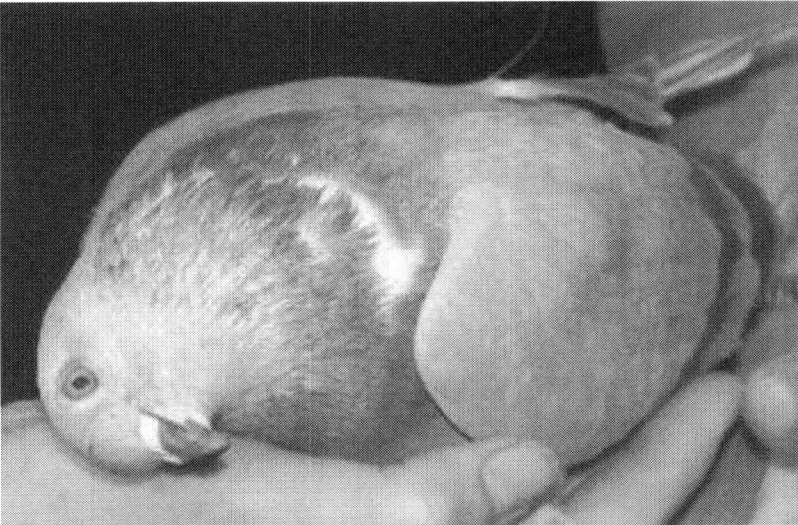

One of the easiest ways to prevent Paramyxovirus from coming into your loft is to try as much as possible to always vaccinate your pigeons at least once a year. Try to vaccinate the young pigeons once they are about 4 to 8 weeks of age. The following are some of the symptoms of this disease; the pigeon will be experiencing watery green slimy droppings, also loss of weight, twisting of neck and head, etc. The following are products you can use for prevention and cure:
- You can use PMV1 Vaccine
- You can use LaSota

3. The Trichomoniasis – Canker disease:

This particular disease is caused by a flagellate which is actually living on the mucous membranes of the throat. The symptoms of Canker include loss of appetite and problem digesting. The following are products for cure:
- You can use Ronidazole (Ridzol)(DAC)
- You can use Metronidazole (Flagyl) (DAC)
- You can use B.S. (Belgica-DeWeerd)

4. The COCCI (Coccidiosis) disease:

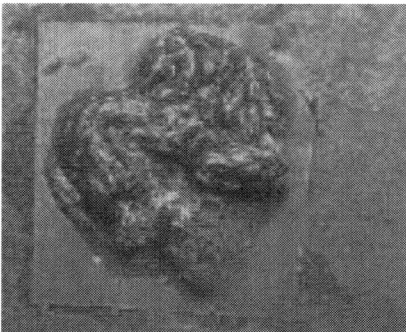

This particular disease in pigeon can be caused as a result of unsanitary conditions in the loft and also when the pigeons are picking around on the ground. The following are some of the symptoms of this disease; poor flying of the pigeon, the pigeon will be experiencing Loss of weight, the pigeon will be experiencing Slimy dark green droppings, the pigeon will be always thirsty, etc. The following are products for cure.

- You can use Multi-Mix (Global)
- You can use Dacoxine 4 in 1 (DAC)
- You can use Trimethoprim/Sulfa (DAC)
- You can use Coccimix (Pantex)
- You can use Cocci-Geel (Pantex)
- You can use Cocci-Mix 1 (Travipharma)

5. The Ornithosis disease:

This particular disease is very common with young pigeons. The following are some of the symptom of this disease; loss of desire to fly, the pigeon will be scratching the head and beak, the pigeon will be experiencing swollen eye lids and wet eyes. The pigeon will be sneezing, rattling and also coughing. The following are some of the products for cure:

- You can use Spiradac (DAC)
- You can use Ornithosis 3 (Belgica-DeWeerd)
- You can use Tylosine (DAC)
- Ornimix DS (Pantex)
- 1 + 1 Cure (DAC)

The following mentioned are the major disease and treatment for pigeons.

PIGEON KEEPING

A GUIDE ON HOW TO REAR HEALTHY PIGEONS

By Lucky James

Printed in Poland
by Amazon Fulfillment
Poland Sp. z o.o., Wrocław